. . . IF YOU LIVED
100 years ago

BY ANN MCGOVERN

ILLUSTRATED BY ANNA DIVITO

SCHOLASTIC INC.
New York London Toronto Auckland Sydney
Mexico City New Delhi Hong Kong

ISBN 0-590-96001-6

Book design by Laurie Williams

12 11 10 9 8 7 6 5 4 3 2 1 9/9 0 1 2 3 4/0

Printed in the U.S.A.
First Scholastic printing, September 1999

CONTENTS

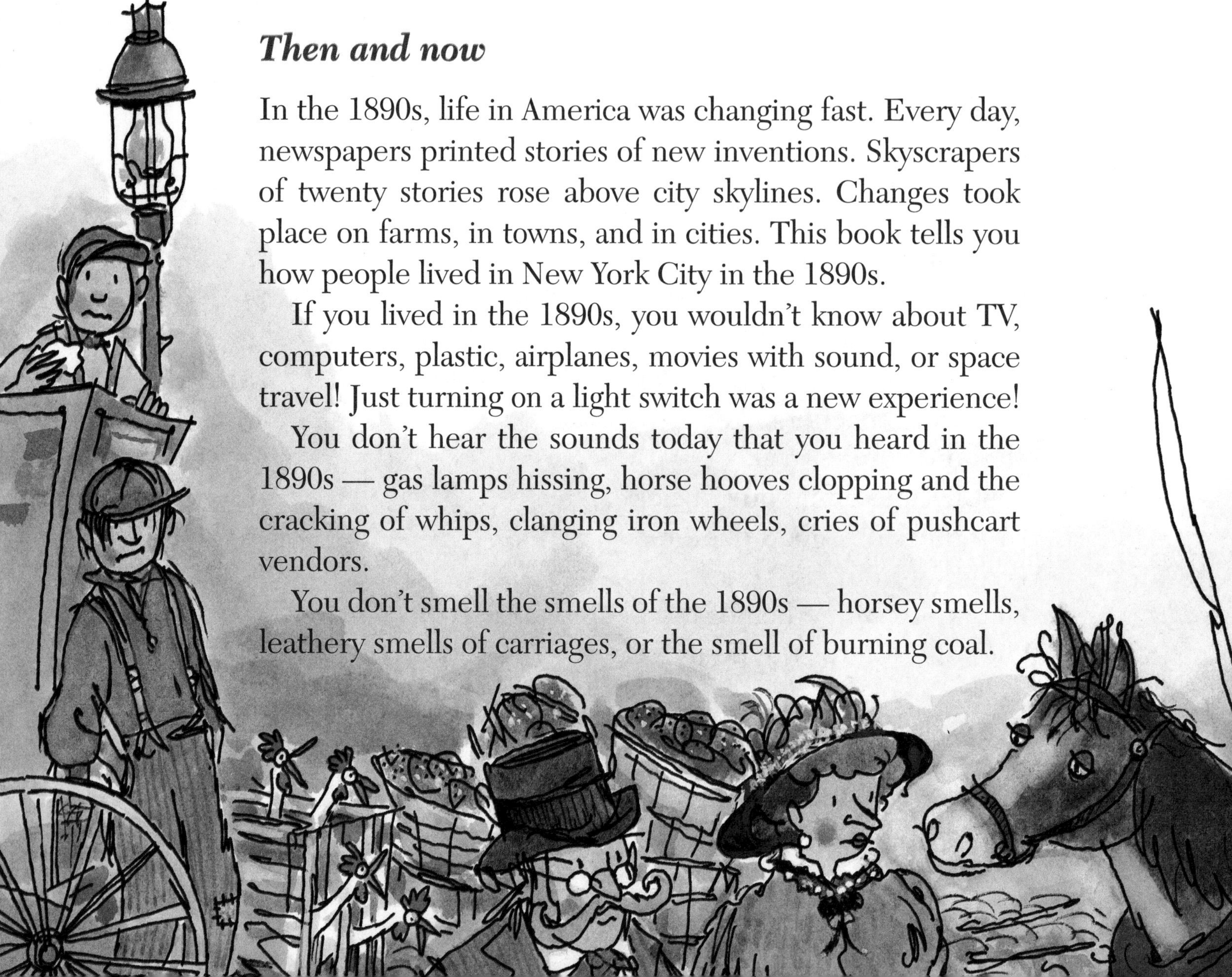

Then and now

In the 1890s, life in America was changing fast. Every day, newspapers printed stories of new inventions. Skyscrapers of twenty stories rose above city skylines. Changes took place on farms, in towns, and in cities. This book tells you how people lived in New York City in the 1890s.

If you lived in the 1890s, you wouldn't know about TV, computers, plastic, airplanes, movies with sound, or space travel! Just turning on a light switch was a new experience!

You don't hear the sounds today that you heard in the 1890s — gas lamps hissing, horse hooves clopping and the cracking of whips, clanging iron wheels, cries of pushcart vendors.

You don't smell the smells of the 1890s — horsey smells, leathery smells of carriages, or the smell of burning coal.

Think about how you got to school today. In 1899, there were no school buses. Think about what you ate today. In the 1890s, there were no pizzas, potato chips, french fries, burritos, or frozen foods. Your life would be completely different.

That time is often called "the good old days." But it wasn't good for everyone. The rich were very rich and the poor were very poor. In the 1890s, there weren't as many people in the middle class as there are today. Middle-class people aren't rich or poor. They are in the middle.

Millionaires made up only a small part of the population. But they had more money than all other New Yorkers put together.

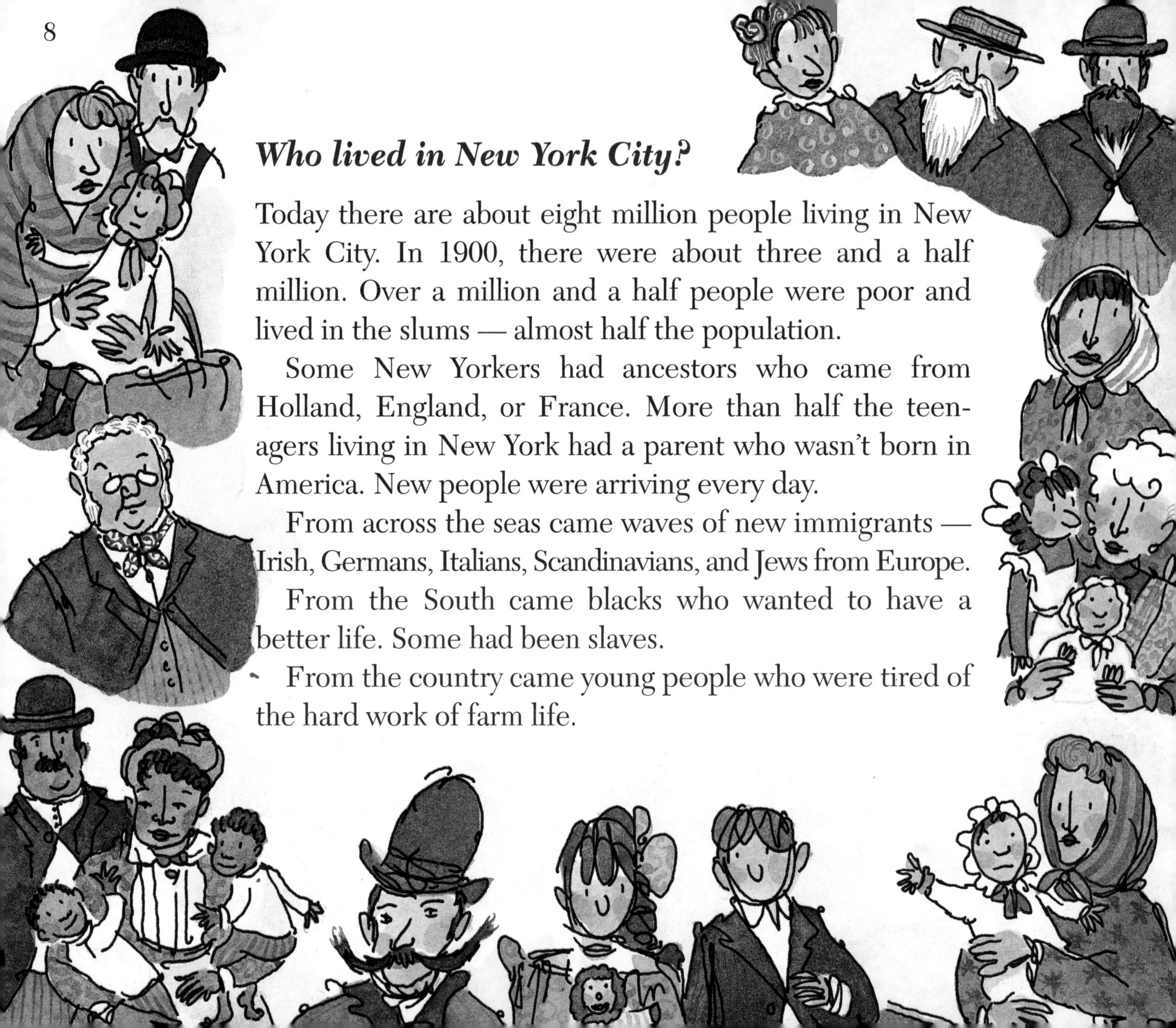

Who lived in New York City?

Today there are about eight million people living in New York City. In 1900, there were about three and a half million. Over a million and a half people were poor and lived in the slums — almost half the population.

Some New Yorkers had ancestors who came from Holland, England, or France. More than half the teenagers living in New York had a parent who wasn't born in America. New people were arriving every day.

From across the seas came waves of new immigrants — Irish, Germans, Italians, Scandinavians, and Jews from Europe.

From the South came blacks who wanted to have a better life. Some had been slaves.

From the country came young people who were tired of the hard work of farm life.

Where did poor people live?

Some poor people lived in shacks made out of junk found in the streets. But most lived in dingy apartment buildings called tenements or in boardinghouses. As many as 2,500 people lived in one block of tenement buildings.

Most tenements had four to six floors. Each floor had four apartments, made up of two or three small, cramped rooms. They did not have fresh air or good light. Rats ran over the floors. Cockroaches crawled on the cracked and peeling walls.

It cost less to live in the back apartments where there was hardly any light.

People in tenements kept their windows shut in winter so they wouldn't breathe in the smoke and soot from factories or smell the odors from stinking garbage. But in the summertime, they had to open the windows for any breeze they could get.

Some rooms had no windows at all. The walls were so thin that you could hear the cries of hungry babies in the next apartment.

Tenement apartments were small and crowded with furniture. Some families had lots of beds and cots for relatives who had just arrived in America. There might also be machines that the family needed to make a living — cigar-rolling machines, sewing machines, or tools for making paper flowers.

The poorest unmarried men lived in shabby buildings called flophouses. It cost a man 25¢ a night for a cot to sleep on, a locker, and a screen to separate him from the man next to him. Just the cot would be 15¢. It cost 10¢ to sleep on the floor.

Boardinghouses were sometimes better than tenements and certainly better than flophouses. A room in a simple boardinghouse was $2 a week, plus $3 extra for meals. (Fancier boardinghouses charged $10 a week for a room.)

People in boardinghouses ate their meals together. A single woman would feel comfortable in a boardinghouse.

Where did the middle class and rich live?

Middle-class people lived in apartment buildings, some with elevators, that were better kept than tenements.

The very rich lived in grand mansions with huge private ballrooms. One house might take up a whole city block.

Rich families were the first to have telephones. The first New York City telephone directory was two pages, with 271 telephone numbers listed. A few years later, in 1880, the directory listed 2,800 names.

Rich people had the newest appliances — gas stoves, toasters, even washing machines. Many had several kitchens and servants to work in them.

The rich had another new invention: toilet paper. Five hundred sheets sold for 50¢. Everyone else used newspapers cut into squares.

Where did people sleep?

The rich slept on soft feather beds in large bedrooms.

The best bed in a tenement was for parents or grandparents. Children shared their bed with brothers and sisters.

Poor children were lucky to have a roof over their heads. Many slept in alleys and doorways and on barges piled high with hay along the docks.

Were there bathrooms in tenements?

There was only one bathroom on every tenement floor, shared by as many as forty people. It was terrible when the plumbing got stopped up.

In older tenement buildings it was even worse. The only toilets were in filthy wooden outhouses in the yards behind the tenements.

In 1901, a law was passed that said all apartments had to have running water and a toilet.

Where did people take baths?

When tenements were built, there were no plans for separate bathrooms. If you had a bathtub, it would be in the kitchen.

In 1880, five out of six houses in cities had no bathtubs. Most likely, you'd take a bath in the public bathhouses.

Big mansions for the rich had fancy bathrooms.

Where did people get water?

One way was to open a fire hydrant on the street and collect water in a pail. If you used the sinks in the hallway, you'd have to wait in line. There were only a few sinks in tenements.

The rich and the middle class had plumbing and sinks. The rich had all the sinks they wanted for their homes.

Would you have electricity?

In the late 1890s, electric lights were slowly taking the place of oil and gaslights in the homes of the rich. Most people could not afford electricity. They still used smoky kerosene lights. Most people didn't have electricity in their homes till the 1900s. Before then:

Your mother would cook on a coal range.

Ironing meant using a flatiron, which was heated on the stove.

Dishes were washed by hand.

If you had a rug, it was swept with a broom or a carpet sweeper.

Sewing machines were run by pushing foot pedals.

Your father would use a straight razor to shave.

Clothes were scrubbed in big washtubs and hung outside to dry on clotheslines.

What good were clotheslines?

Clotheslines were not only used for hanging out wash. You could send messages and run groceries to the top floors of tenements.

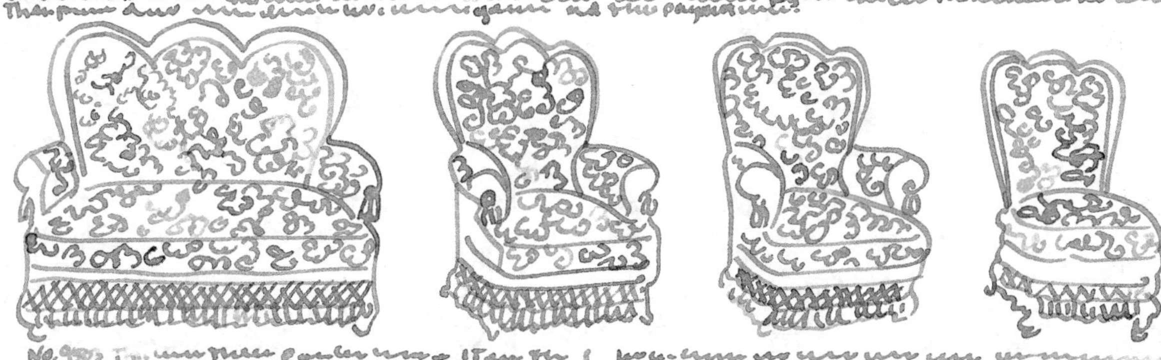

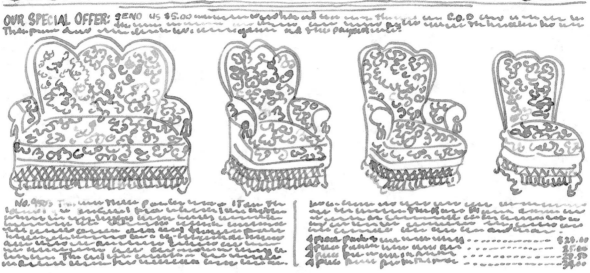

Where did you shop?

Clothes and household items were sold in department stores. Starting in 1872, people could shop in a new way — by mail. Two big stores, Montgomery Ward and Sears Roebuck, printed catalogs with pictures showing everything to wear or use in your home. By 1899, the Montgomery Ward catalog had 1,036 pages.

People shopped on the street. Street vendors sold everything your family might need — from medicines to puppies, from a tin cup for 2¢ to a peach for a penny.

Some street vendors had special cries:

The scissor-and-knife sharpener had a portable grinder. He'd ring his bell and cry, "Razors, scissors, knives to grind."

The fishmonger cried, "Fresh fish fit for the pan. Here comes the fish man. Bring out your dishpan."

The fruitman cried, "Raaaaaaaaaspberrrrrries! Blaaaaack-berrrrrrrries! Fresh berries!"

Milkmen drove around the city in horse-drawn wagons. They sold milk before the sun came up, crying, "Fresh milk."

Men selling old clothes wore piles of hats on their heads.

Umbrella menders, washtub menders, barrel menders, and odd-job workers walked the streets calling out their services.

If you were poor, you might get old, stale food at Saturday night markets. Or you might shop from push-carts.

If you were rich, your servants shopped for you.

How did people keep food fresh?

In an icebox. The iceman put big blocks of ice in the top of the icebox. The ice kept the food below cold. Melted ice water dripped into a tin pan. You had to empty the pan whenever it got full.

In the icebox of a rich person, you'd find meat wrapped in paper and tied with string. Butter, lard, and cheese were packed in paper-thin wooden boxes.

Ice for iceboxes was cut into blocks from frozen rivers. The ice blocks were packed in sawdust and stored in warehouses, where they stayed frozen through the hot summer months.

 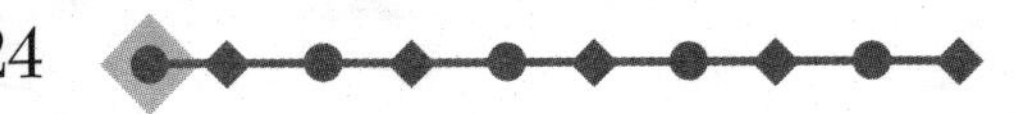

What were some of the new inventions?

By the 1890s, people were using things they had never dreamed of before — drinking straws, chewing gum, zippers, safety pins, bottled Coca-Cola, fountain pens, typewriters, safety razors, postcards, carpet sweepers, and home sewing machines.

In 1899, Orville and Wilbur Wright of Dayton, Ohio, were working on an invention called the airplane. But it didn't fly until 1903.

What did women and girls wear?

Fashions changed every few years. Rich women wore the latest styles.

In the 1890s, most women loved the Gibson girl look. Artist Charles Gibson drew sketches of women wearing blouses with leg-of-mutton sleeves that puffed out at the shoulders and a skirt that came down to the ankles. Women wore uncomfortable corsets to make their waists look smaller. They wore stockings of striped, heavy cotton.

The rich wore fancy dresses of velvets, laces, and furs. Fur muffs kept their hands warm.

They had walking dresses, riding dresses, sailing costumes, dresses for the garden and for playing croquet.

Some of their ball gowns came from Paris. When a rich lady went to the country for a month or so, she might take sixty dresses in large trunks, called Saratogas.

Women wore shoes and slippers with long, pointed toes. They also wore hats — the bigger the better.

For bicycling, women wore high-button shoes and skirts that hid their legs. They always wore hats, even when they biked.

Poor girls wore hand-me-downs or homemade dresses made of cheap material. They wore thick stockings and high-button shoes. Sometimes they'd wear an apron to keep their clothes clean.

Girls loved to wear bows in their hair.

What did men and boys wear?

Boys wore caps and *knickers*, loose pants ending at the knee. A boy wore a large bow tie for special occasions and stuck a handkerchief into his jacket pocket.

Men wore suits over long underwear in the winter. Shirts weren't made with collars and cuffs attached. You'd have to put on stiff starched collars and cuffs.

Men wore silk top hats or bowlers and they always carried a pocket watch.

Men wore knickers when they played golf or went boating.

Men and boys slept in nightshirts.

Photographs of the 1890s show that poor boys sometimes went barefoot on the dirty city streets.

What were bathing suits like?

There weren't any bathing suits. Girls wore bathing dresses that came down to their ankles. Boys swam in sleeveless shirts and tights.

What did men and women look like?

Men parted their hair in the middle. They grew mustaches, which they waxed and curled up at the ends. Older men had huge, drooping "walrus" mustaches. Only a few shaved their mustaches.

Women wore their hair long, frizzled with a curling iron and puffed with rollers. The most popular hairstyle was the psyche knot — pulled back and knotted on top. Women wore beautiful ornaments in their hair.

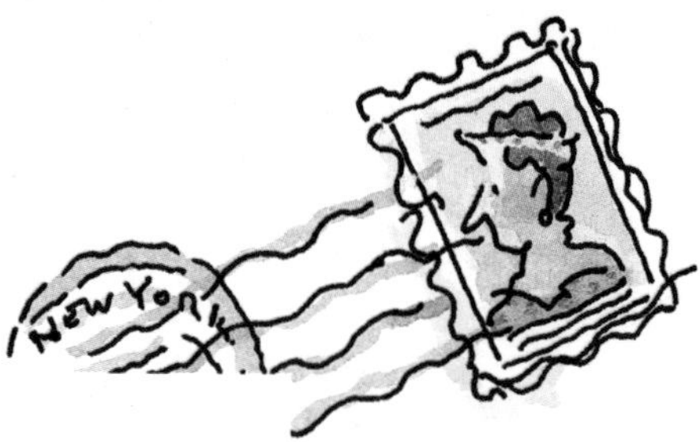

What did things cost in the 1890s?

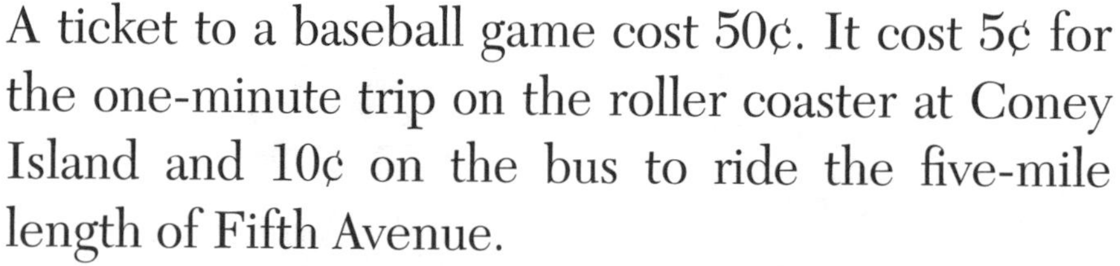

A ticket to a baseball game cost 50¢. It cost 5¢ for the one-minute trip on the roller coaster at Coney Island and 10¢ on the bus to ride the five-mile length of Fifth Avenue.

A clock that ran for eight days without winding cost $7.20. An alarm clock was 60¢ more. A watch was $3.65.

You could get a cheap camera for $1 in 1899. Better cameras sold for $25.

You could get a pair of shoes for $1.95. A new bike cost $14.95. It cost 3¢ to mail a letter.

Did your mother work outside the home?

By the turn of the century, one out of every five women in America worked for pay. Most worked on machines in factories or at home. Others worked as teachers, salesgirls in big department stores, or as clerks and typists in offices. A few women were lawyers, doctors, engineers, social workers, and scientists.

Women were paid a lot less than men who were doing the same work.

Women were shopkeepers, printers, tailors, hatmakers, and chicken pluckers. Ragpickers searched through piles of garbage for anything they could sell.

Rich women did not have to work. But some wanted to improve the lives of slum children and their families. They worked to improve conditions for the poor.

What work did men do?

Men were clerks, teachers, bricklayers, doctors, carpenters, engineers, architects, builders, policemen, actors, shopkeepers, and traveling salesmen called *drummers*.

There were many firemen because there were many fires. Wooden buildings went up in flames nearly every day.

Sandwich men wore signboards on their backs and their fronts. The signboards advertised products from medicines to carriages.

Letter writers wrote letters for people who had never learned to write. Photographers pasted their work on boards to advertise their craft.

People showed and sold the latest gadgets — from type-writers to needle threaders.

A *footman* worked for the rich. He rode outside on the back of a coach. He opened doors for passengers and took care of their baggage.

A *whip* was a coach driver.

A *hackman* drove a carriage or coach for hire.

A *teamster* or *wagoner* drove a horse-drawn freight wagon.

Before the automobile was popular, there were many jobs having to do with horses, coaches, and wagons.

Many men worked in factories. Sometimes factory workers had to work up to twelve hours a day. Factories did not pay workers for overtime. The workers had to pay for their own soda pop because the water from the hall tap wasn't clean. Bosses watched them all the time. If they made a mistake, they had to pay a fine. The fine came out of their weekly pay.

There wouldn't be better working conditions until the labor unions were more powerful — and that was still a few years away.

A *liveryman* took care of horses.

A *blacksmith* made iron shoes for horses.

A *wheelwright* made and repaired wheels for wagons, coaches, and carriages.

Who took care of the children?

Men and women who worked sixty hours a week had little time to care for their children. Youngsters were left by themselves or with a relative — sometimes a sister or brother only a little older. Many poor children had to work.

Where did children work?

Rich and middle-class children didn't have to work. But poor children worked alongside adults in factories. Sweatshops were workplaces squeezed into tenements. Sweatshops were hot and without fresh air so people working there really did sweat. Sweatshop labor was working six, sometimes seven days a week, up to twelve hours a day.

Many children and adults worked at home making clothing, artificial flowers, and cigars. They made twine and paper collars and boxes. They made envelopes and got paid three and a half cents per thousand! They stripped tobacco leaves — a dangerous and harmful job.

Boys worked as bootblacks polishing shoes. Small boys made good chimney sweeps. They could fit inside chimneys to knock down soot with brooms.

Boys sold newspapers on the streets or on horsecars, shouting, "Extra, extra, read all about it!"

Boys worked shoveling coal, cleaning pigsties, and begging. They did all sorts of things to make a few pennies. They did magic tricks, played music on a hand-organ or in a band, delivered packages, ran errands, and carried heavy coal and firewood.

Girls sold matches, toothpicks, cigars, ribbons, candy, shoelaces, and flowers. They sold hot corn out of baby carriages or children's wagons.

What happened to children who didn't have a home?

A great many poor children were homeless. Some ran away from bad homes. Some were orphans without a mother or a father. Some had parents who didn't have enough money to feed them.

Thousands of homeless children lived in shelters run by the Children's Aid Society. They got a bunk, a breakfast of bread and coffee, and a supper of pork and beans.

To keep from starving, some children stole food from carts and crates outside grocery stores.

How old did children have to be to work?

There weren't any laws that said children couldn't work. So many children as young as five went to work.

Between 1880 and 1900, two million to three million children in America didn't go to school. They worked instead.

How much money did people make?

The average pay for a man was 22¢ an hour for a fifty-nine-hour workweek — about $13 a week. Women and children who worked in factories and sweatshops were paid much less. A woman might earn a dollar for every twelve overalls she stitched together.

Children seldom made more than $2 or $3 a week.

Some rich men who were bankers, merchants, or factory owners made millions.

What did people eat?

Breakfast for the poor was mostly bread and tea. Some ate what they could find in trash cans.

Secondhand food markets sold groceries and meats that were sometimes rotten. Some restaurants along the docks sold the food that was left over from people's plates in fancy restaurants. They made stews and soups, which they sold for 15¢ a portion. Hot soup was free in soup kitchens.

People ate food that would not pass a health inspection today.

Fast food — 1890s style — was sold right on the street. You could buy oysters, buns, pretzels, hot-spiced gingerbread, berries, oranges, baked pears, Italian ices, and German sausages.

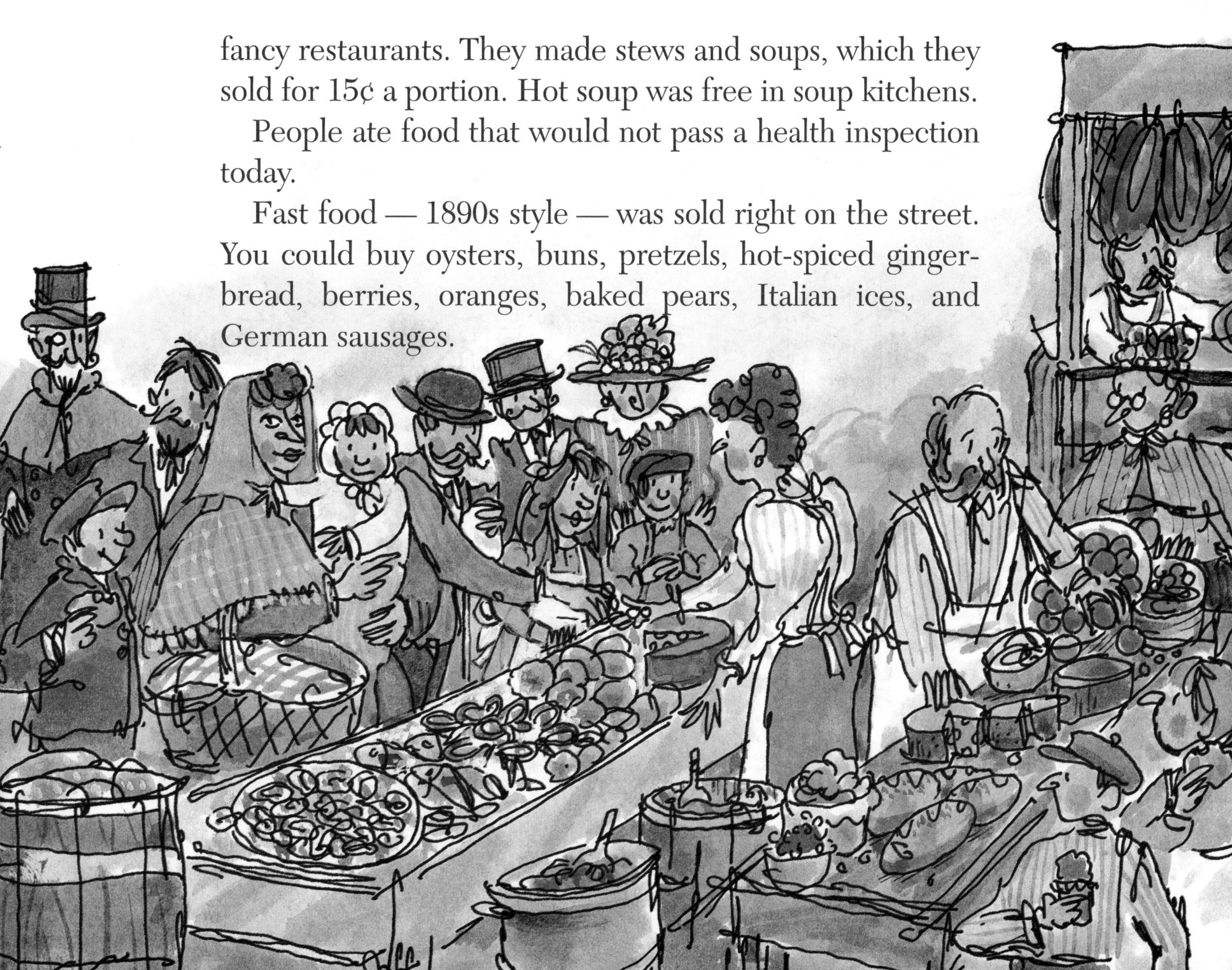

A breakfast in a boardinghouse was big. A typical breakfast was fried mutton chops, fried eggs, and lots of toast with jam and coffee.

The first cold cereals came out in 1895. And in 1896, the first bagel was baked in New York.

What did rich people eat?

A lot. A dinner in a fine restaurant or at home might start with a platter of oysters, then a turtle soup, then a fish dish, then a whole small hen in cream sauce, then lamb, turtle, duck, salad, vegetables, and a sweet dessert like ice cream served in fancy shapes or pears cooked in wine and sugar and swimming in apricot sauce. Some people ate thirteen different courses at dinner.

There were always side dishes — salted almonds and celery stuffed with cheese. A butler and two footmen served the dinner. Children were not allowed to stay up for these dinners. They ate much earlier, usually with their nannies or the cook, and their meals were much simpler.

What did people do for fun?

People went to see plays, operas, and funny shows called vaudeville that played in theaters. They loved to go to Madison Square Garden to see Buffalo Bill's Wild West Show, with its hundreds of horses. The Sportsmen Show had canoe races and water-polo games in a water-filled 150-foot tank.

In the winter, there were sleighing parties and races between iceboats and trains that ran along the Hudson River. The iceboat was almost always the winner. In the summer, people traveled by steamer to the beaches around the city.

What did the rich do for fun?

On weekends they went coaching. Their polished carriages and fine horses paraded through Central Park. Sometimes they sailed in their fancy yachts on the rivers.

The rich ate out in fancy restaurants or went to parties. One society lady gave a dinner party for her pet monkey. One man hired birds to sing in rosebushes that were planted just for the party. Costume parties were popular. One guest wore a suit of armor that cost $10,000. Gold bracelets were hidden in napkins as party favors.

Men went to their private clubs where women were not allowed.

What was fun and cost 10¢ or less?

At the drugstore you sat at the soda fountain and ordered an ice-cream soda for a dime.

Some people had pianos and organs. They had musical evenings where they played the piano and sang. You could buy sheet music, with the printed words and music to the latest tunes.

They danced the lively two-step. Ragtime and folk music were popular in the 1890s. "Carry Me Back to Old Virginny" and "A Hot Time in the Old Town" were big hits. When you went sledding in the winter, you'd sing "Jingle Bells," which, even 100 years ago, was an old favorite.

Children liked the new amusement park at Coney Island. If you didn't want to go on the scary rides, you could always play in the sea wearing the latest style bathing costume.

You could visit the zoo in Central Park or hear concerts on Saturday afternoons. It was fun to skate on park ponds in the winter. Central Park was the first big park built in a city. It opened in the winter of 1859.

You could go to a dime museum.

What was a dime museum?

A dime museum cost 10¢ but it wasn't really a museum. It was a place to see strange things. There were fire-eaters, sword swallowers, fat ladies, midgets, snake charmers, bearded ladies, four-legged chickens, and a room called the Chamber of Horrors filled with ghastly things.

What games would you play?

You'd play chess and checkers, kick the can, and hide-and-seek. Mumblety-peg was a boys' game. A boy would throw a knife toward the ground trying to make the blade stick. There were kites, marbles, spinning tops, magic tricks, and lead soldiers.

You might play tiddledywinks, Parcheesi, and Pillow-Dex, a kind of Ping-Pong. Instead of the little white ball, a balloon was batted over a net on the table.

Girls liked dolls. In 1880, the inventor Thomas Edison made the first talking doll.

Cat's cradle was played by arranging string in different patterns over a partner's hand.

You and your friends made many of the toys yourselves. You'd read *The American Boys Handy Book* and *The American Girls Handy Book*. You'd learn how to raise frogs; stuff a bird; take care of your bicycle; start a club; make telephones out of boxes, paper, and string; make paper daisy fans, corn-husk dolls, and much more.

Were there movies?

In 1896, a small crowd watched the first moving picture flicker across a screen. Two girls danced with umbrellas, and two men boxed in a funny boxing scene. The movie

showing ocean waves breaking on the shore was so real that people sitting in the front row were afraid they would get wet!

But there was no sound — no talking. The early movies were called “flickering flicks.” Many people went to the silent movies every week.

Where did poor children play?

Poor children had to work long hours, so they didn't have much time for playing. The tenements were too far from Central Park and there were hardly any other parks in the city. Children played in the hallways, on the roofs, in the streets, and they swam in the East River.

Poor children might not have the nickel fare to ride the trolley to the beach or to the new amusement park at Coney Island.

They couldn't even buy a five-cent ticket to the circus. Some sneaked into the circus tents.

It was fun to find a Sunday newspaper with the comics printed in color!

Were there sports?

When basketball began in 1891, it was played with a soccer ball and two baskets.

You might play the new game of volleyball. There was baseball and stickball, bowling and tennis, football and boxing, golf, archery, and skating.

What was the most popular sport?

Bicycling. By 1896, there were four million bicycle riders in the country. There were two-wheelers, three-wheelers, and bicycles built for two. There were bicycle races and bicycle parades.

 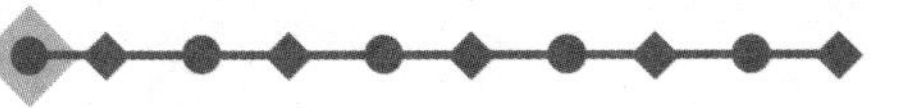

How did people get around in the city?

Not by car! In 1895, there were only eight automobiles in the entire country. The next year there were sixteen. By 1899, there were 2,300, and by 1900, there were 8,000 cars in the United States. But it would be some years before the streets were filled with autos.

Elevated railways known as "els" rumbled above the main avenues of New York City. They were twice as fast as horsecars.

Passengers riding the el could see into third-floor apartments. The people living on the third floor had to close their curtains for privacy.

The first underground subway wasn't completed until 1904.

In 1900, horses were still pulling trolleys. But the next year, horses were replaced by electric trolleys.

It took three horses to pull a double-decker bus along the five miles of Fifth Avenue. It took an hour and a half to ride up and down the avenue. On hot evenings, people rode the bus just to cool off.

If you wanted to go from Manhattan to Brooklyn, you'd cross the new Brooklyn Bridge, the longest suspension bridge in the world, which opened in 1883. It was said to be one of the wonders of the world.

What did most people think about the new automobiles?

They didn't think much of them. Cars were called "horseless carriages." They broke down a lot and didn't have the power to climb hills the way horses did. You didn't have to change tires on a horse! Car tires usually wore out after 1,500 miles.

"Get a horse!" was a slogan heard around the country a hundred years ago.

What were the streets like?

Garbage sometimes piled up four feet high. One visitor said that New York City looked "like a huge, dirty stable."

The main streets, such as Broadway, were a mess of noise, dirt, horse manure, and traffic — horse-drawn trucks, carts, wagons, and coaches. Two-wheeled delivery carts were driven by wild drivers in white coats.

The first electric streetlights were turned on in 1880, but traffic lights weren't used until 1919. Before then there were always traffic jams. When the police were called in, they used their clubs to stop fights and runaway horses. They helped old people cross the street and got the traffic moving again.

The streets were so bad that an expert was hired to solve the problem. The first law he made said no carts and horses were allowed to stand in the street overnight. Stables were built for all the horses.

He organized a street cleaning department in 1895 to clean up the 60,000 gallons of horse urine and the two and a half million pounds of horse manure in the streets every day! The cleaners wore white uniforms.

By 1898, most of the main streets were made of hard asphalt. Other streets were still covered with rough broken stones called *cobblestones*.

Were the horses treated well?

Not always. Many drivers beat them and rode them hard until they fell over. Tired horses pulled heavy, crowded streetcars and buses. Horses sometimes trampled over one another and many were left to die in the streets.

Horses were treated so badly that people formed organizations to protect the animals. They set up watering stations where horses could get a drink.

Were you comfortable riding in a carriage?

No way! One traveler wrote that he was “tossed about like potatoes in a wheelbarrow.” Some roads were so rough that you could be thrown out of your seat. If you were riding on the roof, you could tumble onto the road.

And sometimes your coach would turn over!

The best seat inside a coach was the one right behind the driver. Though you'd have to ride backward, you wouldn't get bumped so much.

What were good riding manners?

Lists of manners were printed in the newspapers:

- **Bathe your feet before starting out.**
- **Don't spit inside the coach.**
- **Take two heavy blankets with you; you will need them.**
- **Don't swear, nor lop over on your neighbor when sleeping.**
- **Don't grease your hair before starting or dust will stick there.**
- **Don't imagine for a moment you are going on a picnic; expect annoyance, discomfort, and some hardships. If you are disappointed, thank heaven.**

Were the railroads any better?

Not much.

People worried that cars would slip off the track or that the boiler would explode. The racket of the railroad cars would give people headaches, and they'd get burned from ashes and cinders flying out of the locomotive's smokestacks. Trains were powered by coal.

But trains were faster than horse-drawn carriages. Trains clickety-clacked at twenty to thirty miles an hour, more than twice as fast as a stagecoach. You could get from New York to San Francisco in only six days. A stagecoach took six months.

By 1900, almost 200,000 miles of tracks crisscrossed America.

How did the rich travel?

In great luxury. George Pullman designed fancy railroad cars for the rich with velvet armchairs, big picture windows with curtains, and colorful stained-glass ceilings.

You'd sleep in a fancy sleeping car lighted with oil lamps. You'd have a private bathroom and sleep on fresh sheets. Before you went to bed, you'd put your boots out. In the morning, a railroad worker called a porter would give them back to you, cleaned and polished. He'd bring you hot water for washing up.

You'd dine in a fancy dining car. You could order five different kinds of bread, four kinds of cold meats, six hot dishes, eggs cooked any way you wanted, fresh fruits and vegetables, and plum pudding.

Did people travel by boat?

Steamboats burned wood that produced steam, which turned huge paddle wheels. In winter, steamboats might sink in ice floes. The rest of the year, they often got stuck on floating branches. Boilers exploded in huge fires.

But there were some luxury boats, too. By the turn of the century, some riverboats were so fancy that they were called "floating palaces." Up to 600 people could travel in luxury.

There were showboats carrying traveling theater groups and floating circuses. They made stops up and down the rivers.

Sailing ships, steam-powered freighters, and ferries sailed into the port of New York every hour.

What slang did people use?

An important person was called a *big bug*.

If you did well in school, your teacher might say, *Bully for you*.

If you were a classy dresser, you'd be called a *dude*. If you were a fast runner, you'd go faster than *greased lightning*. Anyone who showed courage or toughness was *full of grit*.

If you got mad about something, you'd *get into a pucker*. If your teacher was a woman, she'd be a *schoolmarm*. If you were making a commotion, you'd be *waking snakes*.

What did people read?

Children read thrilling adventures in paperback novels that cost a dime. They also read good books — *The Story of a Bad Boy*, *The Adventures of Tom Sawyer*, *The Adventures of Huckleberry Finn*, *Little Women*, and *Black Beauty*.

The Wizard of Oz was published in 1900.

Children read a magazine called *Golden Days for Boys and Girls*. They looked at the pictures in *National Geographic* and in *Frank Leslie's Illustrated Newspaper*.

Besides their Bibles, almost everybody read an almanac, a book of facts about everything under the sun. People read the almanac to find out next year's weather.

You'd read "wish books," the mail-order store catalogs. You could order any of the thousands of items for sale and it would come in the mail.

And if you didn't have a book or a magazine, you could read the thousands of posters and signs in the streets.

How did people advertise their products?

The streets were filled with signs that advertised everything — painless dentists, food, medicines, and songs. There were so many signs — big, wide, and tall — that finally a law was made. Signs could be no higher than two feet.

Advertising posters were hung on fences, garbage cans, walls, and vacant lots.

Wooden signs hung in front of stores. Shoemakers used the sign of a boot, hatmakers used the sign of a hat, and a gilded watch advertised a jeweler. Life-size wooden Indians holding cigars were the signs of cigar shops; red-and-white-striped poles, ten feet high, were the signs of barbershops.

There were advertisements in newspapers and magazines, too.

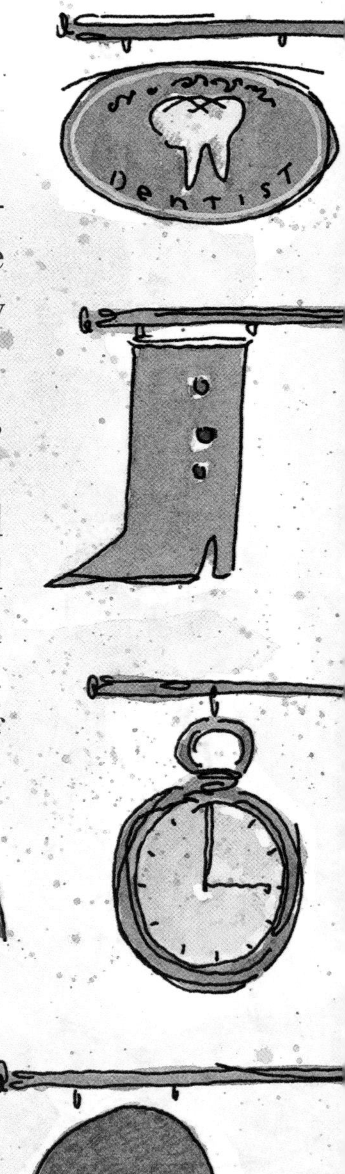

Who went to school?

Every child was supposed to go to school. But poor children needed to work to help their families. Some children who worked during the day tried to go to night school. But they were so tired from working all day that they often fell asleep.

It was worse for black students. There were special schools for blacks only, with very few classroom supplies. The average amount of schooling a black child had in a lifetime was 100 days.

The rich were taught at home by private tutors or they went to private schools.

What were public schools like?

Many were terrible! They were overcrowded, filthy, and poorly lit. Schools that were built for 1,000 children often had twice that many.

Sometimes there would be 100 or more students in a classroom. Desks had to be shared by two or three children. Schoolbooks were shared, too.

In one school in the slums, there weren't any benches or chairs. The children had to sit on the dirty floor. There were no playgrounds.

What were teachers like?

They didn't have much training. Some children knew more than their teachers.

Teachers drilled facts and figures into their students. They used the rod and switch to punish them.

Some teachers didn't try to break up violent fights between the children. They were afraid to get in the middle of boys who were biting and slugging each other and throwing stones.

If women teachers got married, they were fired. But it was okay for a male teacher to be married.

What did you learn?

You learned to spell better than you learned to think. You learned by memory, repeating your lessons over and over. If you were a good speller, you were considered a good student. The more facts you knew, the better grades you'd get.

If you were good at *oratory*, you were good at public speaking. You would memorize long poems and famous speeches and recite them at school assemblies. You might join a debating team. In a debate, you would take one side of a subject and try to make it interesting. The person you were debating presented an opposite point of view. The speaker who got ideas across the best was the winner of the debate.

Your schoolbook was *McGuffey's Reader*, filled with stories, poetry, adventure tales, and bits of Shakespeare. Stories often had a moral message. One message was that if you did good deeds you would end up with a good job.

What happened if you got sick?

Often you'd be better off not going to a hospital. Operations weren't always safe. Doctors knew little about germs. Their instruments were often rusty. They didn't even wear masks or gowns when they operated.

Were there any good doctors?

Most people didn't trust doctors — with good reason. Almost anybody could practice medicine without proper training. And there was almost nothing doctors knew how to do for a patient in pain. Medicines often did more harm than good.

Doctors were paid up to $3 for an office visit and $6 for a house call. No wonder country doctors moved to the cities. In the country, they only got 50¢ for a house call.

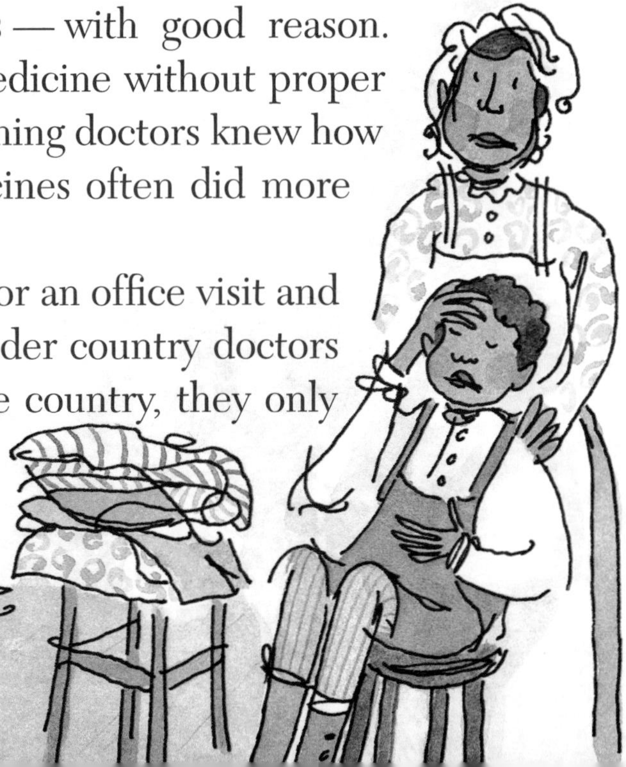

Diseases spread from slums to other areas of the city. Most doctors didn't understand that germs were spread by filth. Between 1870 and 1900, 45,000 New Yorkers died from diphtheria, a terrible illness.

The poor who got sick were sent to overcrowded and filthy "poorhouses," almshouses, or public hospitals.

Were there nurses?

Before 1880, people treated nurses like servants. Through the work of Florence Nightingale, nurses began to be well trained and more respected.

What kinds of medicines did people use?

There were powders, potions, pain remedies, and promises of miracle cures.

You wouldn't need a prescription for patent medicines. You could buy them by mail or from the druggist. Thousands of patent medicines were said to cure any sickness. The people who made them and sold them became rich. The people who bought them didn't know what was in them. Some contained alcohol and drugs that could be dangerously habit-forming.

When did life for the poor get better?

Not all rich people were selfish. Many cared about the poor. A newspaper reporter, Jacob Riis, wrote a book called *How the Other Half Lives*. Riis's photographs showed people living and working in miserable conditions. Men and women who cared about the way the poor lived began to work for changes.

They started settlement houses where poor people had classes in health and education. The poor could even take baths in bathtubs! They could listen to music and see paintings.

In the 1900s, laws were finally passed to protect children. New laws said all children under the age of fourteen had to go to school. There were laws that called for better housing, safer foods and medicines, shorter working hours, and improved public schools. Things began to look up for many people.

More people of the middle class began to enjoy new inventions, such as washing machines, that made their lives easier. More and more people bought furniture and clothing made in factories.

Many could afford to ride the trolley out to the countryside and the beaches. The new century — the twentieth century — was a time of hope for many.

How do you think life will change in the next hundred years?